MAGNIFICENT
GRACE

MAGNIFICENT GRACE

EMBRACING THE GREATNESS OF GOD

Margaret Feinberg

Foreword by Patsy Clairmont

THOMAS NELSON
Since 1798

NASHVILLE   DALLAS   MEXICO CITY   RIO DE JANEIRO

Published in Nashville, Tennessee, by Thomas Nelson. Thomas Nelson is a trademark of Thomas Nelson, Inc.

Thomas Nelson, Inc., titles may be purchased in bulk for educational, business, fund-raising, or sales promotional use. For information, please e-mail SpecialMarkets@ThomasNelson.com.

Unless otherwise noted, all Scripture quotations are taken from THE NEW KING JAMES VERSION. ©1982 by Thomas Nelson, Inc. Used by permission. All rights reserved.

Scripture quotations marked NIV are taken from HOLY BIBLE: NEW INTERNATIONAL VERSION®. ©1973, 1978, 1984 by International Bible Society. Used by permission of Zondervan Publishing House. All rights reserved.

ISBN: 978-1-4185-4931-2

Printed in China

11 12 13 14 RRD 5 4 3 2 1

Contents

Contents

Foreword

My husband Les and I moved into our home in Franklin, Tennessee a year ago. In Michigan, our birth state, our small town held a handful of church choices; but in Franklin there are a plethora of steepled offerings. The street corners literally chime with glorious hymns and rhythms of faith. As we've church shopped in this land of plenty, it has been delightful to visit various congregations and to see first-hand what God is doing in the extended body of Christ.

Recently someone asked where I attend. As I rattled off the churches we've visited, it sounded like every church had the word "grace" in its name. With a laugh I quipped, "Tennessee has too much grace." But, really, can one be offered too much grace? I think not.

Grace makes space for frail humanity's faults . . . without passing judgment. Really stop for a moment and dip your life-weary heart into those still waters. Rather than eye-rolling, finger pointing, or balling a fist over our mess ups, grace extends open arms and pure intentions. She allows us room to breathe deeply, calming us all the way down to our tippy-toes and all the way up to our churning thoughts. What relief to exhale our tension and inhale God's hospitality! Grace doesn't revel in shaming; instead, she delights in redemption's quiet work—no matter how long it takes. Offering peaceful boundaries, sound counsel, and deep comfort, grace is a lady with her wick trimmed and her lantern lit.

We all long for the companionship of grace, for our journeys can be arduous. Wait, did I say "can be"? I meant they inevitably are. We can't skip through this life without tripping over trouble, skidding into scandal, or sinking into the muck of life's tedium. And when we are up to our eyelids in sadness, sorrow, and regret, only grace can walk in and make space for us at the table of restored hope and dignity.

My dear friend, Carol, when diagnosed with breast cancer initially responded as many would with tears and much trepidation. But then grace appeared. Carol knelt and sipped deeply from the grace cup and then rose up to move through her journey with unexplainable courage and deliberate gratitude. Not gratitude for the disease, but for those who extended kindness to her in the midst of the battle: everyone from nurses aids to the neighbors who brought casseroles throughout her ordeal benefited from the transformation.

I remember when Carol chose to shave her head before cancer took that choice away. She was brave. She was beautiful. She stayed close to laughter, to her faith, to her family, and to purposed conversations of love. Even her last breath was full of grace's legacy.

I don't know the map of your story, but like mine it probably leads up mountains of great joy and through valleys of despair. The good news is grace signs up for the whole journey, empowering us to do more in heartbreaking places and everyday spaces than we could have imagined.

Can one be offered too much grace? I think not!

—PATSY CLAIRMONT
JUNE 2011

Introduction

Grace Like Rain

Grace is the gift of Christ, who exposes
the gulf which separates God and man,
and, by exposing it, bridges it.

KARL BARTH,
THEOLOGIAN

When was the last time you felt the first light pitter-patter of cool raindrops on your skin? The sensation probably sent you looking for the closest dry area you could find. If there wasn't one nearby and the drops began to multiply, you may have found yourself drenched.

In some ways, grace is a lot like rain. Sometimes it catches us by surprise. We find ourselves sprinkled with grace when we least expect it. Other times it falls in an outpouring that drenches us in the reality of God's goodness and love. Like rain, grace can be both life-giving and cleansing.

The grace God gives is not meant to stop at us; it's meant to be poured through us as we become more grace-filled and graceful. When we receive God's magnificent grace and realize the wonder of the gift, we can't help but extend it to others.

Grace gives the strength to face imperfections and faults, knowing that God's provision is greater than human lack. Grace gives the ability to extend kindness when circumstances might tempt us to withhold it. Grace welcomes us into a deeper relationship with God—no matter where we've been or what we've done in the past. Indeed, grace is amazing!

Throughout this study, we'll look at different facets of God's grace in our lives. We'll consider the abounding grace God gives us, though sometimes it's hard to wrap our minds and hearts around such a lavish gift. We'll examine portraits of grace from throughout the Bible, focusing on people who not only experienced God's grace but exhibited it in their attitudes and actions. We'll also look at demonstrations of grace in our lives, marveling that God can send grace like a summer shower that catches us off guard with refreshment and replenishment.

My prayer is that you'll find yourself rediscovering the wonders of God's grace throughout this study. I hope that as you do, you'll find yourself encouraged to extend grace to others.

Blessings,

Margaret Feinberg

Abounding
in Grace

Grace has a way of catching us by surprise. God extends

this amazing gift to us, His children, in countless ways

so that we will abound in grace in every area of our lives.

One

Sufficient Grace

*No one is safe by his own strength, but he
is safe by the grace and mercy of God.*

CYPRIAN,
CHRISTIAN WRITER

From the beginning, God lavished us with His grace. In Genesis we read of God's creation of the earth, the moon, the sun, and the heavens. God placed each star in the sky for our enjoyment. He designed beautiful flowers and unique animals for our wonderment.

Then, at the peak of creation, God made man and woman in His likeness.

His creation was good, and mankind was *very good*.

God gave the man and woman (named Adam and Eve) a beautiful garden as their home and made them stewards over the rest of His creation. The role came with only one rule: the first couple could eat and enjoy every fruit in the garden except for that which grew on the Tree of Knowledge of Good and Evil.

All was well until a crafty and manipulative serpent approached the woman, enticing her to enjoy the forbidden fruit and reap its benefit: to possess the same knowledge as God.

Eve bit into the fruit before convincing Adam to do the same. As they savored the tangy juice on their taste buds, their eyes were opened. For the first time, they realized they were naked. They felt shame. They experienced fear.

Life in the garden was no longer perfect. Sin entered the scene.

God poured out abundant grace on Adam and Eve, just as He continues to pour out His grace on us today.

God could have chosen to start over with His creation. Taken away free will. Designed something different. One could argue that's what Adam and Eve deserved.

Instead, God poured out abundant grace on Adam and Eve, just as He continues to pour out His grace on us today.

When Adam and Eve hid in their nakedness, God created garments out of animal skin—the first sacrifice made on behalf of human sin. Then, like any loving father, God disciplined His children. He listed the repercussions for their disobedience.

The woman would have increased pain in childbirth. The man would toil to cultivate the now difficult ground. Strife would emerge in their relationship. They both would eventually die.

The Lord disciplines those He loves, but He also extends grace. God's grace toward humanity is displayed in the curse on the serpent. In Genesis 3:15 God said, "He shall bruise your head, and you shall bruise His heel." In Hebrew, word translated as "he" in this verse doesn't describe all of humankind, but is actually a singular, masculine pronoun. The reference alludes to a specific man who would defeat sin once and for all: Jesus Christ.

Tempted by the serpent, Adam and Eve allowed sin to get the best of them. This was not the end of the human story but rather the grand beginning. In God's love, mercy, and grace, He created a plan for redemption that extends to all who accept it.

Adam and Eve may have deserved death, but God gave them something they didn't deserve: grace. Not based on merit, grace is a free gift that is completely unearned. God didn't just extend grace to Adam and Eve but to all humanity through the death and resurrection of Jesus Christ, which cleanses us from sin. From the beginning, God established a plan for redemption, a powerful expression of grace to all of His children, through His Son, Jesus.

1. *How would you define grace?*

2. *What challenges your ability to accept and embrace God's grace in your own life?*

3. *Read **Genesis** 3. According to verse 6, what three things caused Eve to respond to the temptation of the fruit? How do these three things tempt us today?*

4. Read **Genesis 2:16–17**. How did Eve's response to the serpent
(Genesis 3:2–3) compare to what God actually said regarding
the fruit? What did the serpent promise Eve would happen if she
disobeyed God?

5. When in the last month have you succumbed to temptation?
Pinpoint the temptation's appeal. What were the consequences of
your action? How did you experience the grace of God through the
situation?

Bible scholars believe the apostle Paul wrote a total of four letters to the church in Corinth, two of which we have in our New
Testament. In his letters, we learn that Paul, one of the founders of
the early church, faced a challenge not unlike those we encounter.
2 Corinthians 12 zeros in on Paul's personal struggles and afflictions.

6. Read *2 Corinthians 12:1–10*. *Paul experienced a thorn in his flesh. What would you identify as a thorn in your flesh right now?*

2 Corinthians 12:7 says, "And lest I should be exalted above measure by the abundance of the revelations, a thorn in the flesh was given to me, a messenger of Satan to buffet me, lest I be exalted above measure." The Greek verb *edothe* meaning "was given" is used here in the passive tense to explain that God gave Paul the thorn in his side. Through it, God kept Paul unable to boast in himself. Some scholars believe the thorn was a physical illness, an enemy, or a group of false apostles. While the exact meaning is unclear, Paul was readily aware of his weakness. God assured Paul that His grace was sufficient. The Greek word *arketos* used for "sufficient" means "enough."

7. *Reflecting on past "thorns" you've experienced, describe a time when God's grace proved sufficient for you.*

8. *How, over the upcoming week, can you actively celebrate God's sufficiency or ability to be enough in your life?*

> *From the very beginning, God lavished us with His grace. As we continue to grow in faith, we further understand God's grace as sufficient in our lives.*

Digging Deeper

In his letter to the church in Philippi, the apostle Paul expressed what happens when we learn to trust that God's grace is sufficient. He explained that he had learned contentment in all situations. Read **Philippians 4:10–13**. What role might grace play in helping us be content in all circumstances, too? How often do you allow thoughts of God's grace to play into your overall satisfaction? What situations are most likely to strip you of contentment? Fill you with contentment? How might you actively choose contentment in a tough situation you face?

Bonus Activity

Over the course of the next week, record in a journal or online diary all instances when you experience God's grace. Note times when the unmerited favor of God is displayed in your home, work, and relationships. Share highlights with the group the next time you gather.

Two

Abundant Grace

Grace is the free, undeserved goodness
and favor of God to mankind.

MATTHEW HENRY,
ENGLISH THEOLOGIAN

Dr. Charles Finney—a well-known evangelist from the Second Great Awakening—spoke at a church in Detroit, Michigan, one Sunday. Finney preached from 1 John 1:7: "The blood of Jesus Christ His Son cleanses us from all sin." As Finney's voice reverberated over the pews, one man was particularly struck by the message.

After the service, this stranger approached Finney and asked if the preacher would walk him home. Finney could tell the man had been through the ringer, so to speak. He certainly didn't look like the average churchgoer: his breath reeked of alcohol, and his fists were cut and bruised. Knowing the man's reputation, church officials wanted to discourage Finney from being alone with him. However, Finney ignored their warnings and began the walk to the stranger's home.

After walking for a while, the stranger led Finney into the back of a building and locked the door. Startled, Finney began fidgeting as he second-guessed his decision to come along.

The stranger reassured him. "Don't worry. I am not going to hurt you." He went on to explain to Finney that they were in the back of his saloon—a place from which he made sure no patron left without becoming completely inebriated. Though mothers and wives had begged him not to serve their sons and husbands alcohol, he never listened.

Finney was filled with compassion and sadness over the hopelessness this man felt.

The man asked Finney, "Could God forgive a man like that?"

Overwhelmed by the story, Finney drew from his earlier message: "The blood of Jesus Christ His Son cleanses us from all sin."

Not convinced, the stranger went on. "I don't just own a saloon. I also own a gambling hall." He described how he made sure every patron left with empty pockets—scammed out of their last dollars.

"Could God forgive a man like that?"

Finney replied, "The blood of Jesus Christ His Son cleanses us from all sin."

The stranger spoke again. "That's not all. I have a wife and daughter who have bruises and scars from my brutality. I haven't said a kind word to them in five years. Could God forgive a man like that?"

Finney was filled with compassion and sadness over the hopelessness this man felt. Once again he answered, "The blood of Jesus Christ His Son cleanses us from all sin."

After their conversation, the man unlocked the door and let Finney leave. For hours the stranger stayed in the room—pouring the alcohol down the sink and ripping up all the cards in his gambling hall. He chose to believe Finney's words.

When he made his way home that morning, the stranger spoke kindly to his wife and daughter—telling them that they had a new husband and father. The stranger became so involved in the church that he later became one of its leading officials. First John 1:7 became his motto. He finally understood grace.[1]

Sometimes we all need a reminder of God's grace, an understanding that nothing and no one is beyond God's redemption. The stranger in the story was completely lost and drowning in sin, but he learned the greatest lesson of all: Jesus died in order to pay the penalty for all sin. In believing that truth, we find freedom.

1. Describe a time when you felt completely trapped in an unhealthy lifestyle or habit. What finally set you free?

In ancient Jewish culture, asking for your inheritance before your father was dead was a cruel slap in his face. The request came across as, "I wish you were dead." Luke 15 describes the story of a son who made such a request and found himself living a self-destructive lifestyle.

2. Read **Luke 15:11–13**. What was the younger son's attitude toward his father when he left his house? Think of a time when sinful desires blinded you. In what ways did your attitude toward family and friends mirror that of the son?

After his funds ran dry, the youngest son was forced to take a job feeding pigs. This detail is significant because swine were despised and untouchable to the Jewish people (Leviticus 11:7 and Deuteronomy 14:8). The son's job, then, was dishonorable. When the young man reached a point where he dreamed of eating the pig's food out of desperation, he finally realized he'd rather be a slave in his father's house than continue catering to swine.

3. Read **Luke 15:14–24**. Place yourself in the younger son's shoes. How do you think he expected his father to react to his return?

In a move that surely shocked Jesus' listeners, the father in the story ran to meet his lost son. In the Jewish culture, a father usually waited to be addressed by a child; but this father pursued his son and welcomed him with open arms. The father was overjoyed to have his son home once again. Rather than expressing displeasure and censure, he lavished his boy with grace and unconditional love.

4. *How does this story impact your understanding of grace? How has the Lord, represented as the father in this parable, surprised you in His forgiveness and grace?*

This parable is often referred to as "The Prodigal Son," but it could also be called "The Begrudging Brother." At the story's close, we learn a little more about the older brother in the story and discover the issues he faced. Interestingly, Jesus used the older brother to symbolize the Pharisees and scribes to whom He spoke.

5. *Read* **Luke 15:25–32**. *In what ways do you relate to the older son? Have you ever rejected or put limitations on God's grace? If so, explain.*

6. *The two sons took very different approaches to life, each other, their father, and grace. On the chart, circle the words in each line that best describe you. Do you relate more to the older son or the younger? Explain.*

Lost Son	Older Son
Left home	Remained home
Prodigal	Productive worker
Squandered inheritance	Celebrated inheritance
Felt unworthy	Confident of worthiness
Recognized sinfulness	Felt righteous
Repented	Resented

7. *Which of the two brothers do you think most needed to experience grace? Why?*

8. *What most often prevents you from running into the Father's arms and accepting His free gift of grace?*

Sometimes we all need a reminder of the abundance of God's grace—a grace that has no limits.

Digging Deeper

When God extends abundant grace toward us through repentance, He doesn't keep a record of our past mistakes. Read **Psalm 103:11–12**. Describe a time when you began to grasp the unfathomable love of God. What does it mean to you to have your sins removed as far as the east is from the west? How has radical forgiveness changed your life?

Bonus Activity

Read **Luke 15** this week. In a journal, write down what you learn about grace from the three parables about things lost and then found. Share what you learn with the group the next time you gather.

Three

Undeserved Grace

*Don't be troubled when you meditate on the
greatness of your former sins, but rather know that
God's grace is so much greater in magnitude that
it justifies the sinner and absolves the wicked.*

CYRIL OF ALEXANDRIA,
ANCIENT CHURCH FATHER AND THEOLOGIAN

God's grace extends to everyone. While some of us are willing to receive it, we struggle to extend grace to others. Even those of us quick to extend God's grace to those around us sometimes find it difficult to lay hold of this precious gift for ourselves. Take the following quiz to discern how you experience and express grace.

The Grace Quiz

1. *You walk into a meeting five minutes late and a coworker walks in ten minutes after you. Just as he did at your arrival, the leader takes time to repeat everything that's already been said. You respond by:*

a. Patiently listening to the leader because hearing information a second time is always helpful.

b. Wondering why the leader is taking valuable time to repeat what's already been said twice.

c. Feeling bad because everyone else who was there on time must listen to the instructions three times.

2. You get caught in rush hour traffic and notice that the left lane is closed due to construction. You make your way to the right lane, but notice a car speeding behind you in the left to bypass as much traffic as possible. You respond by:

a. Waving the car around you, reasoning we're all in a hurry sometimes.

b. Blocking the car's path and hoping the driver will find it difficult to merge.

c. Dwelling on all the moments you've done something similar and annoyed drivers around you.

3. Exhausted after a long day, you finish shopping at the grocery store and head to the ten items or less self-checkout line. As a station opens, a lady with a full cart cuts in front of you. You respond by:

a. Remaining silent and offering to help bag her groceries.

b. Complaining to the attendant that she has too many items for self-checkout and giving her a cold stare.

c. Remembering all the times you have inconvenienced others by taking a long time to check out.

4. You run an extra load of laundry because you spilled dinner all over your favorite dress last night. As you finish up, you see your young niece carelessly spilling bright red juice all over her white shirt. You respond by:

a. Helping your niece change, laughing off the mess, and quickly putting stain remover on the shirt.

b. Stepping away to avoid growing angry with your niece.

c. Remembering all the times you have ruined clothes because of your clumsiness, and figure it must run in the family.

5. The month of September is busy for your family. You forgot to send your sister-in-law a birthday card. After calling to apologize for the oversight, you learn your spouse forgot his sister's birthday, too. You respond by:

a. Dialing her number for him that night so he can wish her a happy birthday.

b. Getting annoyed that he forgot his own sister's birthday. He should be the one reminding you.

c. Recalling all the important dates you have missed over the years.

Score

If you answered mostly As, you easily extend grace toward other people. You understand that life sometimes gets in the way and often give grace when you can. You also have a healthy understanding of the need for grace in your life.

If you answered mostly Bs, you easily receive grace from other people. Life may not always go the way you plan, but you are happy when others extend you grace. Reciprocating grace may not come naturally for you. By growing more aware of moments when you receive grace, you are better equipped to know how to extend it.

If you answered mostly Cs, you are learning to understand the meaning of grace. While you extend and receive grace on occasion, you may still wrestle with the idea that grace is not something deserved. Be encouraged that you can't do anything to earn God's grace.

The wonder of God's magnificent grace is that though we do things that may make us seem unworthy of it, we are still able to experience it. Since the grace we receive from God is undeserved, we must be willing to extend grace to others whether or not we feel they deserve it.

1. *Consider your responses to the quiz. Do you tend to be better at extending grace or receiving it?*

2. *Think of an extremely gracious person you know. Without using his or her name, list attitudes and actions you associate with that person.*

3. *When in the last month have you had difficulty receiving grace? Extending it?*

Sometimes it proves difficult to extend grace, especially when we have been wronged. Jesus often used parables or stories to teach His followers; and in Matthew 18:21–35 He offered a startling teaching on forgiveness and grace through a story demonstrating the consequences of unforgiveness and a lack of grace.

The lesson began when Peter approached Jesus and asked Him how often he should forgive. Judaism recommended forgiving a transgressor up to three times, thus proving a spirit of forgiveness, whereas the further need to forgive a person would suggest he or she was unrepentant, simply pretending to be sorry for what happened. Peter, then, likely thought himself generous in offering to forgive others seven times, more than double the culturally suggested number. Some scholars believe Peter chose the number seven to symbolize completion.

> *Jesus makes it clear that we're meant to forgive others and to continue forgiving them.*

4. Read *Matthew 18:21–22*. How well does your willingness to extend grace and forgiveness to those who hurt you match Jesus' admonition to forgive as often as needed?

Jesus makes it clear that we're meant to forgive others and to continue forgiving them. He illustrates this idea by telling the parable of the unmerciful servant.

5. Read *Matthew 18:23–27*. How does the master extend grace? Describe a time when someone did something similar for you.

A talent was not a coin but a weight measurement defining money's worth. One silver talent was worth about six thousand denarii. One denarius was equal to a day's wages. In other words, the first servant owed an unfathomable amount of money.

6. Read *Matthew 18:28–35*. In the chart below, compare the first servant's debt with the second servant's. Which is the worst debt? According to the debt load, whom would you expect to be first to extend grace and forgive the debt?

First Servant's Debt	Second Servant's Debt

7. Why is it important to be intentional about receiving grace? Extending it? Explain the connection between the two concepts.

8. How in the next week can you be more intentional about receiving grace freely and without conditions? What changes might you need to make in order to make sure you extend grace to others in the same way?

As we begin to recognize and appreciate the grace God extends us, we can more fully extend contagious grace to those around us.

Digging Deeper

One way we can extend grace to others is by being quick to forgive. Read **Colossians 3:13**. When in the last month were you faced with a situation requiring forgiveness? Describe your response to the incident. What factors made it difficult to forgive? Why do we often make excuses and put conditions on our forgiveness? How does forgiveness relate to grace?

Bonus Activity

Think of three personal situations where forgiveness and grace are currently needed. Pray—take a step to forgive those who hurt or disappointed you. Ask God to help you extend grace and receive it as needed. Record in your journal your thoughts along the way.

Four

Saving Grace

God doesn't just give us grace, He gives us Jesus, the Lord of grace.

JONI EARECKSON TADA,
CHRISTIAN AUTHOR

The cross provides the ultimate picture of grace. Jesus didn't have to die a painful death. The Son of God didn't have to suffer. Jesus didn't have to lay down His life for the unworthy and undeserving.

But He did.

Jesus endured a painful death on the cross—one completely undeserved—for us. The cross provides a beautiful example of sacrificial love. Jesus loved us so much that He was willing to give His life so that we could live. He died an undeserved death to save an undeserving people, who cannot earn His love or His grace.

Today's lesson is all about your story. What does the cross mean to you? Fill out the chart using each letter of the alphabet to begin a word or phrase that, for you, captures the meaning of the cross. Maybe thoughts of the cross bring to mind a memory or a specific person. A Scripture passage or hymn. Be creative. You may want to write an adjective, a place where you lived or worked, or an experience when Jesus' work on the cross made an impact on you.

A	
B	
C	
D	
E	
F	
G	
H	
I	
J	
K	
L	
M	
N	
O	
P	

Q	
R	
S	
T	
U	
V	
W	
X	
Y	
Z	

Jesus' action on the cross is the ultimate example of God's free gift of grace—His blood poured out so that we will stand righteous in God's eyes. By reflecting on the times in our lives when the cross was most meaningful to us, we develop a better picture of grace.

> 1. List in order of significance the top three favorite memories, moments, or words you recorded in the alphabetical chart.

Luke, the author of the gospel by the same name, also wrote the book of Acts. Following the Gospels, the book of Acts provides a history of the early church as well as a collection of adventure stories, including the riveting accounts of a shipwreck and a miraculous escape from jail. Foremost among the many men and women remembered within its pages are Peter and Paul. Acts 16 recounts the details of Paul's missionary journey to Macedonia with his friend, Silas.

2. *Read Acts 16:16–40. How did the jailer experience the saving grace of Jesus Christ?*

3. *Do you know anyone who has experienced saving grace through a miraculous event? If so, describe their situation. Do you think it's necessary to have a dramatic experience to come to belief in Jesus? Explain.*

4. *Look up the following passages. Record what each passage reveals about God's gracious gift of salvation.*

Scripture	Revelation about Salvation
Romans 3:23	
Romans 6:23	
1 John 5:11–13	
1 John 1:9	
Romans 10:9–10	

In his letter to the church in Ephesus, Paul summarizes his understanding of salvation through grace.

5. *Read **Ephesians 2:8–10**. What comfort do you find in knowing that you're saved through grace instead of works?*

6. *In what situations are you most tempted to think you must work for your salvation instead of relying on the grace of God?*

The Lord knows we are forgetful. That's why in the Scriptures, God often assigned specific tasks meant to spark memory. In order to remind us of His faithfulness and grace, for instance, He invited us to participate in communion.

The apostle Paul wrote 1 Corinthians to the church in Corinth, giving them instructions on ministry and faith. In chapter 11, Paul addressed and scolded the church for their improper usage of the Lord's Supper, a special meal first demonstrated by Jesus to remind people of His sacrifice. At that time in Corinth's history, a large social gap lay between the rich and poor. Out of this came the tendency within the church to exclude from participation in the sacrament those who could not afford to contribute to the communion meal. Paul wrote to remind the church what was truly important.

7. Read *1 Corinthians 11:18–32*. Describe a time when communion was particularly meaningful to you.

8. List three ways you can be more intentional about remembering the grace and salvation offered by God through Jesus.

We are saved by grace—God's saving grace demonstrated through Jesus' sacrifice on the cross.

Digging Deeper

Read the initial story of the Lord's Supper celebrated in **Matthew 26:26–29; Mark 14:22–26;** and **Luke 22:14–20.** What similarities and differences do you note among the gospel accounts? How, according to 1 Corinthians 11, does this picture of communion differ with Corinth's version? With how communion is celebrated today?

Bonus Activity

Over the course of the next week, read the crucifixion scenes in the four gospels (**Matthew 27:32–56; Mark 15:21–41; Luke 23:26–49; John 19:16–36**). Prayerfully record in a journal any details that stand out to you. Spend time thanking Jesus for His incredible sacrifice.

Portraits
of Grace

God's grace has been on display since the beginning of

time. The Scriptures provide account after rich account

of what grace looks like in the lives of those He touches.

Five

Grace Remembered

We need to develop a kind disposition,
to be sensitive to others and truly desire
their happiness. But sensitivity alone is
not enough: the grace of goodness impels
us to take action to meet those needs.

JERRY BRIDGES,
CHRISTIAN AUTHOR

The Bible tells us that Saul was the first king of the Israelites. Chosen by God to lead the people, he was anointed by the prophet Samuel. But it wasn't too long until the power went to Saul's head, and he began disobeying God's commands. Often acting rashly, Saul brought trouble to Israel.

Meanwhile, during a battle between the Israelites and the Philistines, a young shepherd named David slayed the giant Goliath using just a sling and a few stones. Saul was impressed, and after the battle, he put David in charge of much of the army. Not long after that, David became best friends with Saul's son, Jonathan. In time

David—not Jonathan, the supposed heir—would ascend to Saul's throne.

The close of 1 Samuel describes a fierce battle between the Israelites and the Philistines, who continued to prove a dangerous enemy. During the Battle of Mount Gilboa, Jonathan and two of his brothers were killed. Devastated, hopeless, and knowing his time of leadership was coming to an end, Saul fell on his own sword.

At the news of the deaths, the nurse taking care of Jonathan's young son, Mephibosheth, picked up the little boy and rushed to get out of Israel. As she hurried to leave, the five-year-old fell, unable to walk. In the same period in which he lost his dad and grandpa to battle, Mephibosheth lost the use of his legs.

King David chose to do something extraordinary. He extended grace toward Mephibosheth.

Orphaned and crippled—both conditions marginalizing him in the eyes of ancient society—Mephibosheth also faced the possibility of being destroyed simply for his family tie to the late King Saul. In ancient times, whenever a new dynasty took power, it was not uncommon for the new king to kill every rival or opponent to the throne, including the family members of the previous king. King David, however, chose to do something extraordinary. He extended grace toward Mephibosheth.

After David accepted his role as the king of Israel, he deeply desired to show kindness and honor the memory of his friend Jonathan. Calling for anyone left of the household of Jonathan and Saul, David soon learned about Mephibosheth.

David wanted to meet his close friend's son and had him brought to his throne room. Out of kindness, he extended mercy and grace toward Mephibosheth and his family. As king, David returned to

Mephibosheth the land that once belonged to Jonathan and Saul and invited him to eat at the king's table.

Mephibosheth was taken aback by David's offer. "Me? A crippled orphan—eating at the king's table? That can't be true!"

But David ignored Mephibosheth's doubts and commanded Ziba, who had been Saul's servant, to serve Mephibosheth and his family.

David was not required to show kindness to Jonathan's son. He didn't have to ensure his well-being or take care of him. No one expected him to extend VIP treatment. In fact, he could have dismissed him completely. But David showed Mephibosheth grace, demonstrating that he truly cared. Though David owed Mephibosheth nothing, David called him into his own royal presence and gave him a glorious inheritance. The scene is not unlike what God in His grace does for us.

1. *Describe the last time you felt compelled to express God's grace to someone. How did you respond? What was the result of your action?*

Mephibosheth's name can be translated as "destroying shame." His story is one of unlikely restoration.

2. Read *2 Samuel 9:1–13*. What three things does David promise Mephibosheth (Hint: verse 7)?

3. On the continuum, circle the answer you think best describes David's promises to Mephibosheth. Which of the three promises David made was the most meaningful to Mephibosheth? Why?

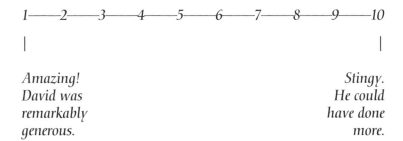

1———2———3———4———5———6———7———8———9———10

Amazing!
David was
remarkably
generous.

Stingy.
He could
have done
more.

4. How did Mephibosheth react to David (verses 6–8)? Have you ever felt disqualified like Mephibosheth? If so, explain.

In 2 Samuel 9:7, David said to Mephibosheth, "I will surely show you kindness for Jonathan your father's sake." Years prior, David, whose name means "beloved," made a promise to Jonathan, whose name means "gift of God." David vowed never to cut off kindness to Jonathan's family (1 Samuel 20:14–17). True to his word, David extended grace to Jonathan's son. He looked at Mephibosheth and both recalled and acted on his love for his friend.

5. *How did the way David looked at Mephibosheth parallel the way God chooses to look on those who place their faith in His Son?*

David's gifts to Mephibosheth were based not on his actions but on grace. Not only did Mephibosheth receive kindness, his land inheritance was restored. He gained access to and fellowship with the king.

6. *What similarities do you see between David's gifts of grace to Mephibosheth and God's gifts of grace to you?*

7. *Does anything about the kindness and grace of God make you hesitant to receive them? If so, explain.*

8. *In what areas of life do you sense God moving you from indifference to compassion? What role might grace need to play in those situations?*

Through the story of David and Mephibosheth, we see a picture of how the Lord extends grace to everyone— even the most unlikely and undeserving. Even to us.

Digging Deeper

In his letter to the church in Ephesus, Paul emphasized the grace given to us through Jesus Christ. Read **Ephesians 1:4–10**. What does it mean to be holy and blameless? What implications should those two descriptive terms for Christians have in your life? How does grace factor into living in a holy and blameless manner?

Bonus Activity

As quickly as you can, list in your journal everything for which you are thankful. Don't be shy. Thank God for creation, your family, your dog, and best of all—for Jesus. Each day this week, return to this entry and praise God for His abundant blessings in your life.

Six

Grace Strengthened

*Trying to do the Lord's work in your own
strength is the most confusing, exhausting,
and tedious of all work. But when you
are filled with the Holy Spirit, then the
ministry of Jesus just flows out of you.*

CORRIE TEN BOOM,
HOLOCAUST SURVIVOR

Picture the strongest man you've ever seen. Multiply his muscle mass by ten, adding to his scalp a mane of thick, long hair. Can you picture it? If so, you are close to imagining Samson, whose life is chronicled in the book of Judges.

Samson's story is found among a history of the judges, special prophets appointed by God to lead the Israelites out of oppression in the years prior to their demand for a king—the first of whom was King Saul. Throughout this book, the Israelites disobeyed God. As a result, God led them into the hands of their enemies, but He sent judges to deliver them after their repentance. (It's interesting to note that several prominent women are recorded among the judges who played significant roles in Israel's history.) Judges 13—16 records the life of one particular judge known for his long hair and undefeatable strength. Samson, whose name means "sun," was a man selected by God to do great things for Israel, God's chosen people.

An angel of the Lord foretold Samson's birth—a miracle in itself because Samson's mom was barren. In the coming years, the boy was raised under the restrictions of a Nazirite vow—one which dedicated him to the Lord physically, spiritually, and mentally. Samson had it all. The strength. The hair. The confidence. The Spirit of the Lord. The God of the universe on his side. But he had one major weakness: women.

Samson was a man selected by God to do great things for Israel, God's chosen people.

The first woman for whom he fell was a Philistine, and the Philistines were by then already the enemy of the Israelites. Samson's Philistine wife proved to be out to trick Samson, and it wasn't long before their marriage fell apart. Before long, Samson moved on to a prostitute in Gaza. Involvement with Delilah followed: she proved the most dangerous temptation of them all. Delilah, whose name means "one who weakened," allied with the Philistines to discover the source of Samson's great strength.

Delilah repeatedly tried to seduce Samson into revealing his secret. At first Samson lied, telling Delilah that if anyone tied him with seven bowstrings, he would grow weak.

Delilah followed Samson's instructions and became angry when the bowstrings didn't destroy Samson's strength and he was able to set himself free.

Again Delilah enticed Samson to reveal his secret. Again Samson lied, telling her that if anyone tied him up with new ropes, he would be rendered powerless.

Again Delilah attempted to take away his strength, but Samson easily broke through the ropes.

Twice more Delilah coaxed Samson to reveal his source of strength. Finally, he told her the truth: "If you cut my hair, my strength will leave."

Judges 16:19 reports that Delilah lulled Samson to sleep in her lap and called a man to shave his head. Samson awoke to the Philistines surrounding him, and this time he could not get free—his strength had been completely drained and he was imprisoned by his enemies. Despite Samson's weakness, God still chose to use him. When he prayed and begged God to strengthen him one last time, God answered. In his final moments, Samson managed to defeat thousands of Philistines in an unforgettable feat of strength.

Samson's story reminds us that God is truly the source of all our strength, too. Further, it testifies to His magnificent grace, because even though Samson made foolish decisions, God still heard his prayer and offered him another chance.

1. What wisdom for life can you draw from Samson's story?

*2. Read **Judges 13**. How did Manoah and his wife respond to the news of a future child?*

The angel of the Lord said that the son of Manoah and his wife would be a Nazirite. The word in Hebrew, *nazir*, means "one who is consecrated or separated."

*3. Read **Numbers 6**. According to this passage, what are the requirements of a Nazirite?*

In following the Nazirite vow, Samson grew to have incredible physical strength, an asset that would help him fulfill the prophecy that he would "deliver Israel out of the hand of the Philistines" (Judges 13:5).

4. Next to each passage, describe the feats that demonstrate Samson's strength.

Scripture	Strength of Samson
Judges 15:8	
Judges 15:15–16	
Judges 16:3	
Judges 16:6–9	
Judges 16:13–14	

In spite of the supernatural ability God gave him, Samson lost sight of the calling to remain holy and set apart. He traded God's gift of strength for the physical affection of a woman who cared nothing for his God. The decision cost him everything—his physical ability, his sight, and even his life.

5. Read *Judges 16:1–21*. How do you think Samson felt as he sat in prison blind and weak?

6. Read *Judges 16:22–31*. How did God display His grace in response to Samson's prayer?

7. Other than women, what were Samson's greatest weaknesses? Greatest strengths? Which of the weaknesses you listed do you share with Samson?

When Samson came to a point where he recognized that he could do nothing on his own, he called out to God, and the Lord gave him renewed strength.

8. *When in the last three months has God given you special strength just when you most needed it?*

> *Even when we feel at our weakest, God's grace is our source of strength.*

Digging Deeper

Hebrews 11, which revolves around a list of men and women who displayed incredible belief in God, is commonly referred to as the "Hall of Faith." Read **Hebrews 11:32–34**. Are you surprised to find Samson mentioned here? Why or why not? How does seeing his name among the faith heroes encourage you in the journey of living as a woman of faith?

Bonus Activity

Over the upcoming week, search for the word "strength" in the Bible. An online search engine like Biblegateway.com or a concordance makes it easy. Journal about what each passage reveals about God's strength and your own. Prayerfully reflect on areas in which you need to rely more on God's strength and less on yours.

Seven

Grace Recovered

*And you know, when you've experienced
grace and you feel like you've been forgiven,
you're a lot more forgiving of other people.
You're a lot more gracious to others.*

RICK WARREN,
PASTOR AND AUTHOR

Years ago Billy Graham was driving through a small town when a siren-blaring police car pulled up behind him. When the officer approached Graham's car, he informed him that he had been driving forty in a thirty mile per hour zone.

Graham quickly apologized. "I'm guilty," he said. "How much is the fine?"

The policeman told him that the fine was ten dollars, and Mr. Graham would be required to appear in court.

In this particular small town, the local court convened in a barbershop. The judge was both justice of the peace and a barber. When Graham walked in, the judge was busily giving a haircut. After he finished with the customer, he assumed his judicial role and called the court to order. He looked at Graham and asked, "Guilty or not guilty?"

"Guilty," Graham said.

"That will be ten dollars—a dollar for every mile you went over the speed limit," the judge announced before realizing that the man standing before him was well-known evangelist, Billy Graham. "You have violated the law, and the penalty must be paid," he said.

Graham reached for his wallet, but the judge protested, "The fine must be paid, but I'm going to pay it for you."

In that moment the judge removed ten dollars from his own pocket and attached it to the ticket. Then he took Graham, whom he had listened to on the radio for many years, out for a steak dinner.

Years later, as he reminisced about the story, Graham said, "That's how our heavenly Father treats repentant sinners."[1]

Graham's story is a wonderful illustration of grace. Though he was clearly guilty of speeding, Graham received the judge's mercy. Instead of requiring him to pay the fine, the judge paid it for him. All of us are guilty of various sins that require penalty; Jesus paid the ultimate price to cover our mistakes.

At times, we may wonder whether something we've done requires more forgiveness than God could extend, but that's what is so amazing about His grace: God gives it to us freely and in abundant measure. Grace falls like rain and seeps into the most unexpected crevices of our lives, purging, healing, and bringing hope for a fresh start. Sometimes this grace is delivered to us through the most unexpected people.

> *All of us are guilty of various sins that require penalty; Jesus paid the ultimate price to cover our mistakes.*

1. *When did you last receive grace despite a mistake you made?*

2. *Describe a time when you made a mistake from which it seemed impossible to recover. What made that mistake seem so unforgivable?*

King David was as a man with a heart set on following God. His name meant "beloved," and he was beloved by God as well as by many who have read his story. Though David's life is marked by greatness, painful missteps marred his journey. While his mistakes could have defined David's life, they refined him instead.

3. Read **2 Samuel 11**. *Give special attention to verse 1. In light of the whole chapter, why do you think David chose not to join his men? What might this reveal about his priorities?*

David made a royal blunder. Rather than admitting his error, he tried to cover up the mistake. Modern newscasters might call the event "Bathesheba-gate."

4. Read **Leviticus 20:10**. *According to this passage, what was the punishment for adultery? How might this have influenced David's actions against Uriah? Does this in any way justify what David chose to do? Explain.*

5. *Describe David's cover-up plan. When have you tried to cover up your mistake? What happened as a result of your efforts?*

Instead of allowing David to get away with his cover-up, God sent the prophet Nathan to confront the king—a very difficult but necessary job. Nathan was the main religious leader at the time, and he was responsible for helping King David to discern the will of God. The prophet had to show bravery and boldness to rebuke the king in his wrongdoing.

6. *Read **2 Samuel 12:1–14**. Over what situation did a "Nathan"—someone who held you accountable for your actions—confront you? How did you respond?*

7. *Describe a time when you had to be a "Nathan," lovingly confronting a friend about a mistake. How did they respond?*

Despite David's mistake and attempted cover-up, Nathan made it clear that David was forgiven (2 Samuel 12:13).

8. *What encouragement do you find in knowing that nothing is beyond God's ability to forgive? For what do you need grace in order to recover and move forward?*

Grace is truly an amazing gift. When we stumble, we can recover through God's grace.

Digging Deeper

David's first child with Bathsheba died, but the two eventually had another son, who became the next king of Israel. Read 2 Samuel 12:15–25. How does Solomon's birth testify to God's redemption? Describe a time when you saw the Lord make something beautiful out of something bad in your own life.

Bonus Activity

Find an accountability partner. Choose a close friend who loves Jesus and talk with her about how you can encourage each other in the faith. Be honest and open about your mistakes. Pray for one another, asking for strength, wisdom, and grace.

Eight

Grace Extended

We believe that the work of regeneration,
conversion, sanctification, and faith is not an
act of man's free will and power, but of the
mighty, efficacious and irresistible grace of God.

C. H. SPURGEON,
CHRISTIAN THEOLOGIAN

Simon (also called Peter) stared into the water, looking for any sign of life. He and his brother, Andrew, had fished all night, but every time the net had come up empty. Peter wiped the sweat off his face with the back of his hand. Then, he heard a voice on the shore.

"Follow me, and I will send you out to fish for people."

Peter wondered, *Who is that Man and what is He asking of us?* But immediately the brothers got up, left their nets, and followed the man who turned out to be Jesus, the Savior of humanity.

Throughout his discipleship, Peter clung to Jesus. He hung on every word. At one point, Jesus even told Peter how He was going to use him to build His church! Needless to say, Peter's allegiance lay with Christ.

But what would happen when that loyalty was tested? When denying Jesus proved easier, even safer than following Him?

By the time Jesus and His disciples sat down to what's known as "The Last Supper," the possibility of Jesus' death was the last thing on Peter's mind. Though Jesus had given many hints that the event was imminent, Peter couldn't fathom that his time of enjoying the physical presence of Christ was speeding to an end.

Peter couldn't fathom that his time of enjoying the physical presence of Christ was speeding to an end.

As they ate and enjoyed one another's fellowship, Jesus again commented that the end drew near. The room grew quiet and the Lord continued, "I shall be with you a little while longer. Where I am going, you cannot come."

Boldly Peter asked, "Lord, where are You going?"

Again, Jesus repeated that the disciples could not follow Him.

Peter responded, "Lord, why can I not follow you now? I will lay down my life for you."

In an answer that likely surprised Peter, Jesus questioned the depth of the man's loyalty. He told him that before the rooster crowed, Peter would disown Him three times.

Aghast and insulted, Peter chose not to believe Jesus' words. Later that night, when Jesus was arrested, many of the disciples decided to flee. Peter, however, stayed close to Jesus, following Him in secret.

A girl approached Peter. "You are not also one of this Man's disciples, are you?" she prodded.

Peter replied, "I am not." The first denial.

Another accusation came: "This fellow is one of Jesus' followers."

Peter answered, "I am not." The second denial.

Again, someone asked, "Were you not with Jesus in the garden? Surely you are one of them, for you are a Galilean."

Peter insisted that this person was mistaken. The third denial.

Just as a nearby rooster crowed, Peter's heart sank as he realized Jesus was right. As predicted, Peter had denied Him three times. His loyalty was not with Jesus fully. How could Peter ever redeem himself?

As it turned out, he could not. Jesus alone could accomplish that.

After His death and resurrection, Jesus extended grace toward Peter on the shore of the Sea of Tiberias. The Lord appeared to Peter and intentionally assured him of forgiveness (John 21).

Just as Jesus offered grace to Peter, He extends grace to us wherever we are on our spiritual journeys. No matter what doubts we have or denying we've done, we need only to call on God to begin receiving His grace.

1. *In what situations or encounters are you tempted to backpedal about what you really believe about God?*

2. *Read* **John 13:33–38.** *Put yourself in Peter's sandals. How would you react to this accusation? Why?*

Interestingly, Peter—likely still stinging from Jesus' prediction—did try to protect Him during the arrest at Gethsemane.

3. Read **John 18:1–11.** *Summarize Peter's actions during Jesus' arrest. Do you think he was attempting to prove Jesus wrong? Why or why not?*

Despite any efforts to prove the contrary, Peter still denied Christ three times—just as predicted.

4. Read **John 18:17–27.** *Why do you think Peter's courage melted so quickly after Jesus' arrest? What factors cause your courage to fade?*

The Gospel of Matthew adds a detail about Peter's denials that John doesn't mention.

5. Read *Matthew 26:75*. Why do you think Peter wept? If cast in a similar situation, would you share Peter's response? Why or why not?

In spite of Peter's denials, Jesus extended him grace—even reinstating him as a follower and giving him a charge to help establish the church.

In one final beachside scene, the resurrected Jesus once again called to His disciples as they fished.

6. Read *John 21*. What do you think Christ meant to teach the disciples by asking them to bring in their fish and then greeting them with a fire built—fish and bread already cooking?

7. *See verse 7. How did Peter react when he realized Jesus was once again calling to him? What does this response reveal about his love for Christ?*

In verse 15 Jesus addressed Peter as "Simon, son of Jonah." Some scholars note this shift in language. Peter, whose name meant "rock," had compromised his relationship with Christ through his denials. Thus Jesus referred to him as Simon until the relationship was reinstated through the fisherman's response to Christ's query. Peter's repeated affirmation led to restoration.

8. *After receiving the gift of grace Jesus extended to him, Peter went on to become one of the church's founders and leaders. How does that knowledge encourage you to commit fully to Christ?*

To begin receiving His magnificent grace, we must only call on God.

Digging Deeper

Peter took Jesus' charge from John 21 and ran with it. On the day of Pentecost, Peter was the first to preach the gospel. Read **Acts 2:14–36; 4:13–20.** How often do you think Peter recalled Christ's forgiveness of his denial? What impact might the memory have made on his life and service to God?

Bonus Activity

Spend time this week memorizing Titus 2:11–13. Write the passage on note cards and place them around your house, car, and workplace.

Demonstrations
of Grace

Throughout His earthly ministry, Jesus demonstrated

grace—often to the most unexpected people.

Nine

Healing Grace

Grace is given to heal the spiritually sick,
not to decorate the spiritual heroes.

MARTIN LUTHER,
THEOLOGIAN

Michael and Jana picked up their six-year-old son, Joshua, from school and noticed a rash on his stomach. Michael decided to take Joshua to the clinic the next day, assuming the doctor would hand him an expensive, smelly cream to clear his son's skin. Getting Joshua to sit still, he figured, would prove the day's biggest challenge.

But when the doctor called Michael into his office, the parent sat in disbelief as words like "hematology" and "children's hospital" met his ears. Joshua had leukemia.

For the next three years, Michael and Jana sought treatment for their son. Rounds of chemotherapy, painful side effects, and overwhelming doctor's bills followed. Michael spent a lot of time simply watching his son, observing his sleep, his brave acceptance of medicine, and his adjustment to life in a hospital bed.

Realizing that God never offered trite explanations for things like cancer, Michael still found himself asking tough questions of God as he wrestled through issues of doubt. Michael began to see that though God could have filled Scripture with lectures on the nature of evil and suffering or waved away our hurts with explanations of how sickness will end in His glory, God did something far better. While He will eventually redeem all our suffering, God used His Word to remind us that He will never cease to invest emotionally with us in the moment. Michael noticed that even in our most difficult times, we can, as Michael put it, "have an acute awareness of Immanuel—God with us."

While He will eventually redeem all our suffering, God will never cease to invest emotionally with us in the moment.

"I thought it would greatly matter to me to know *why* Joshua had cancer," Michael reported, "but especially during the worst days, I didn't really care. What I really wanted was relief, not explanations. [I found that] though God doesn't promise to tell us why, He gives us something better: Who [is there to help us]. And the Who satisfies more than the why ever could."

After more than fifty chemotherapy treatments and three thousand pills, Joshua was cancer-free. And though the fear of a relapse always lurks, Michael and Jana are grateful for every day with their son.

In his book, *Wednesdays Were Pretty Normal*, Michael reflects on the experience, saying, "I've learned that God is faithful to give grace for what you need, even when—and perhaps most especially when—you don't even yet realize that you need it. I had no idea how much grace I would need on the day Joshua was diagnosed; I also had no idea how much grace God had given me for that day.

Perhaps, then, part of not worrying about tomorrow is that you trust that tomorrow, no matter what it brings, will have sufficient grace provided."[1]

1. When have you been surprised by the sufficiency of God's grace?

2. What lessons did you learn through the experience?

Jesus healed countless men and women throughout His earthly ministry, but one of His more controversial healings is found in the Gospel of John. There a series of questions regarding the issue of blindness arises. In ancient Israel, retribution theology—the belief that anything wrong with a person is the result of and punishment for sin—was widely accepted. Yet Jesus challenged this misunderstanding when He extended God's healing grace to a man born without sight.

3. Read **John 9:1–3**. Compare Jesus' reasoning for the man's blindness with that of the disciples.

4. Read **John 9:4–34**. Make a list of challenges the blind man faced throughout this passage. Which do you think were the most difficult to endure? Why?

5. According to John 9:24, what did the Pharisees try to persuade the blind man to say about his healing? What does this reveal about the character of the Pharisees?

6. Read **John 9:35–38**. How did Jesus extend healing grace in this passage? What do His actions reveal about His care for the man?

The blind man received more than physical sight; he received spiritual vision. He recognized Jesus as the Light of the World, the Son of God, the Messiah—the Promised One of Israel. For the blind man, the healing grace of Jesus wasn't just for his body; it was for his spirit, too. Yet despite this powerful evidence, the religious leaders rejected not just the physical miracle itself but its source.

7. Read **John 9:39–41**. Describe a time when you were spiritually blind but had your eyes opened through the truth of Christ. How did the experience change your perspective?

8. In what areas do you sense God's Spirit trying to open your eyes so you can see more clearly and experience His healing grace?

*Part of not worrying about tomorrow means
trusting that no matter what the next day
brings, sufficient grace will be provided.*

Digging Deeper

Jesus extended healing grace throughout His earthy ministry to people with all kinds of afflictions. Read **Mark 10:46–52**. What similarities and differences do you see between this passage and John 9? How does the faith of Bartimaeus challenge you?

Bonus Activity

We all know people who face challenges: physical, financial, emotional, or relational. This week, lift up in prayer those in need of healing. Ask God to reveal His grace and glory in each situation. Write notes of encouragement to friends and family facing difficult times.

Ten

Grateful Grace

*Gratitude changes the pangs of
memory into a tranquil joy.*

DIETRICH BONHOEFFER,
THEOLOGIAN

As World War II came to a close, a multitude of Allied prisoners sat in POW camps across Germany. One camp in particular housed both American and British soldiers. The guards had them completely separated, and they were unable to communicate with one another. The only exception was that every day at noon, the American chaplain and the British one were able to exchange a few words at the fence separating the two groups of prisoners.

Using anything they could get their hands on, the American prisoners put together a barely functioning radio and tried to scour from the air any news they could from home or regarding the war. One day they heard an unforgettable announcement: the German command had surrendered. The war was finally over! The Americans were elated.

The German guards, whose communications had been severed, had no idea of the breaking news. They continued to imprison the soldiers for several days after the actual end of the war. In the meantime, the American prisoners determined to let the British prisoners in on the amazing news. They sent word through their chaplain. Shouts of praise and celebration echoed from the British living quarters.

The American and the British soldiers continued celebrating the news of the victory. During that time, they smiled and waved at their captors—knowing the Germans would soon have a rude awakening.

With grace comes the freedom to lay hold of the life God has for us.

Sure enough, the camp soon received the message. On hearing the news of Germany's loss, the guards fled, and the British and American soldiers left the camp as free men.[1]

The prisoners were overwhelmed with gratitude for their freedom. We can only imagine the joy and delight they felt at the announcement of the end of the war. Similarly, the great news of God's grace invites us to celebrate with enthusiasm and fervor. With grace comes the freedom to lay hold of the life God has for us.

1. *Describe the last time you received a piece of positive news or a gift of encouragement that proved memorable. How did you respond?*

2. *When in the last month have you have forgotten to be thankful? Explain the impact of the oversight.*

3. *When has someone been ungrateful toward you? How did you respond?*

Leprosy, now known as Hansen's disease, is a skin infection caused by a strain of bacteria. Often a person suffering from leprosy has nerve damage, skin sores, and debilitation. In biblical times, anyone suffering from leprosy was considered unclean; as a result, they were forced to live on the outskirts of society (Leviticus 13:45–46; Numbers 5:2–3).

4. *Read **Luke 17:11–14**. Compare the cries of the men with leprosy to Jesus' response to them.*

The one man who returned to thank Jesus had likely spent his life discounted for two reasons: he suffered from leprosy, and he was a Samaritan. Yet Jesus did not disregard this man, choosing instead to heal him physically and spiritually.

5. *Read Luke 17:15–19. Why do you think only one of the men returned to express gratitude for the healing grace received? What might have prevented the other nine from returning to say thanks?*

6. *Whose example do you tend to follow: that of the one leper who expressed gratitude or that of the other nine who didn't? Explain.*

7. Rank the following excuses for not expressing gratefulness in the order of how often you tend to use them. How might you overcome your primary tendency?

____ I forgot. I got caught up in the excitement of the moment.

____ I lack confidence in knowing whom to thank. Besides, what would I say?

____ I worry so much about results and outcomes that I forget about the source of success.

____ I take good things for granted.

____ I attribute experiences to chance or take the credit for myself.

8. In what areas of life did you once hold a deep sense of gratitude that has faded or waned? How might you intentionally recapture and express thankfulness?

> *It's difficult to receive God's grace*
> *without a deep sense of gratitude.*

Digging Deeper

One genre of the Psalms is that of thanksgiving. In such sections, writers praised and thanked the Lord for His involvement in their lives. Read **Psalm 100**. Do you know someone who embodies this kind of intentional thankfulness towards God? How does her attitude impact your approach to the Lord? In the space below, write your own psalm of thanksgiving to God.

Bonus Activity

List three people in your life whom you tend to take for granted. Over the course of the next week, go out of your way to express thanks and to show them your gratitude in meaningful ways.

Eleven

Generous Grace

Grace is love that cares and stoops and rescues.

JOHN STOTT,
ENGLISH CHRISTIAN LEADER

An impoverished blind man walked his dog in London one evening. He knew he needed to cross the street, but each time he stepped out, he was nearly trampled by passing horses and carriages. Hoping for a break in noise as a sign of a clear path, he waited patiently on the corner.

Thousands of bystanders walked by in those moments, but none offered assistance. Not one stopped his carriage. But then, in what must have proved a great moment of relief for the stranded man, someone grabbed his hand. "Trust me," said a voice. "I'll get you to the other side."

Out of options, the blind man had no choice but to place faith in the stranger. Hand in hand, they walked across the street. When they reached the opposite side, the blind man was filled with thanks. He heartily expressed to the stranger his gratitude for the kindness shown.

As the stranger disappeared inside his carriage and went on his way, bystanders approached the blind man and excitedly asked if he knew the identity of the man who had just guided him across the street. None other than the Prince of Wales, Prince Edward VII, had stopped his carriage to help the blind man cross. Already overflowing with thankfulness at a stranger's simple kindness, the blind man was taken aback: the prince himself took the time to help him—a blind beggar![1]

Even before the blind man knew the identity of his guide, he was filled with gratitude. How much more humbled and thankful did he feel to know that the son of Queen Victoria herself went out of his way to show generous grace.

Just as God has showered His generous grace down on us, we can show generous grace to others in our everyday lives.

Sometimes we think about generosity in terms of receiving a physical gift, but some of the most generous things we can give can't be purchased with any amount of money. Abundant generosity fused with grace empowers us to share God's goodness at every turn. Just as God has showered His generous grace down on us, we can show generous grace to others in our everyday lives.

1. *What surprised you about the identity of the stranger in the story? What similar stories have you heard about a famous person helping someone less well-known?*

Jesus, too, went out of His way to help a man who often went unnoticed. In biblical times, tax collectors were commonly corrupt and, therefore, very wealthy. As a result, society usually despised tax collectors. They tried to disassociate themselves from them. Jesus, on the other hand, sought out Zacchaeus, a despised tax collector, and publicly announced a desire to spend time in his company.

2. Read **Luke 19:1–7**. What does this passage reveal about Zacchaeus' profession, character, and stature?

3. How did the townspeople react to the idea of Jesus addressing Zacchaeus?

4. Imagine this scene taking place in your town. What might serve as the modern professional equivalent of an ancient tax collector? Do you think such an individual would elicit a similar response should Jesus show up and speak with him?

5. Read **Luke 19:8–9**. How does Zacchaeus respond to Jesus? How does Jesus in turn respond to Zacchaeus? Whose response is more generous? Why?

6. Do you think the crowds were more surprised by the words of Zacchaeus or Jesus? Explain.

7. Zacchaeus was a spiritually curious man who had to go to unusual lengths to find room in a very crowded scene. On the continuum below, mark how much room you currently make for people like Zacchaeus.

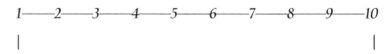

1———2———3———4———5———6———7———8———9———10

| |

I make lots   *I make little*
of room for   *room for the*
the spiritually   *spiritually*
curious.   *curious.*

8. *How can you become more intentional about extending generous grace and making room for the spiritually curious in your life? Workplace? Church?*

> *Abundant generosity fused with an understanding of the grace we've received empowers us to share God's goodness at every turn.*

Digging Deeper

After Jesus met Zacchaeus, He told the parable of minas. Read **Luke 19:11–27.** Usually, Jesus' parables included characters representing individuals or groups. Who do you think each character in this parable represents? Why was the master so happy with the work of the first two servants? Why was he so disappointed with the work of the third? How do you think this parable relates to Jesus giving His disciples a specific task meant to follow His return to the Father?

Bonus Activity

Just as Zacchaeus accepted Jesus' invitation of grace and changed his lifestyle, we can do the same. Over the course of the next week, gather a pile of things from your closets, attic, or garage that you don't need. Donate the items to a local charity. Consider spending a day volunteering and serving those in need in your community.

Twelve

Celebrating Grace

There is nothing but God's grace. We walk
upon it; we breathe it; we live and die by it; it
makes the nails and axles of the universe.

ROBERT LOUIS STEVENSON,
AUTHOR

Imagine yourself visiting a circus for the first time. You look in awe at the bright colors of the giant tent. You smell funnel cakes covered in powdered sugar and notice the tang of cheesy nachos. Performers dressed in vibrant costumes fill the ring. The ringmaster's deep voice booms over the loudspeakers: "Welcome to the greatest show on earth!"

In the coming moments, animals perform tricks. Clowns parade and do wild and funny acts. Cymbals clamor for attention. Zany music rings through the air. A unicyclist whizzes by.

Then the moment everyone has been waiting for arrives—the tightrope walkers emerge. You sit in awe at their balance and grace as they walk, run, and tumble across the small, thin cord hung above the crowd. While gasps fill the air during near falls and missteps, you soon notice a net stretched underneath their rope to catch them. A well-trained, professional tightrope walker will get right back up and try again in the event of a fall.

There is no doubt that the difficult and precarious task of the tightrope walker leaves those who witness it with a sense of marvel. As we determine to live a life in Christ, we, in a sense, walk a tightrope of our own. Like tightrope walkers, Christians are called to walk with focus across situations in a way that can sometimes leave the rest of the world looking on in awestruck wonder.

Christians are called to walk with focus across situations in a way that can sometimes leave the rest of the world looking on in awestruck wonder.

Following Christ means sometimes causing people to crane their necks as they watch our lives and declare in awe, "Look at how well she loves her neighbors and her enemies!" "Look at how beautifully she forgives!" "Look at how selfless and merciful she is!" "Can you believe how she interacts with the needy and the oppressed?" Each step we take provides another opportunity to reveal the truth of who Christ is as we reflect His heart to a world that is watching.

But just as a tightrope walker sometimes slips and falls, followers of Christ do, too. A net of grace, however, always waits to catch us. Both that net and our ability to walk on the wire in the first place are examples of God's grace at work in our lives. Even when we fall, God's grace helps us get back on the rope.

Beautiful high wire performances prompt celebration. How much more should we celebrate a life which reflects God's magnificent grace?[1]

1. *Describe a trapeze or high-wire act you've seen. Would you have the courage to walk a tightrope? Explain.*

2. *Do you know someone who lives life on a tight rope, illustrating by example the kind of compassionate involvement with others that Jesus displayed? What admirable qualities does that person display?*

3. *Describe a time when you fell off the rope and landed in the net of God's grace.*

Jesus' first miracle is recorded in John 2. While a long line of miracles are recorded throughout the gospels, Jesus' first miracle—turning water into wine—hints at the sense of celebration and abundant joy that accompanied those touched by Jesus' life and ministry.

4. Read **John 2:1–5**. *Does anything about Jesus' interaction with His mother surprise you? How does Jesus' mother display trust in Jesus? How difficult or easy is it for you to put your trust fully in Jesus? On the continuum below, mark your answer.*

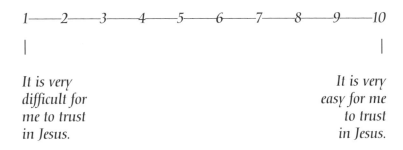

1——2——3——4——5——6——7——8——9——10

|

It is very
difficult for
me to trust
in Jesus.

It is very
easy for me
to trust
in Jesus.

Running out of wine at a wedding was an embarrassing dishonor for the host family. In the culture of Jesus' time, wedding festivals went on for days. Jesus redeemed the situation when He created wine from water.

Jesus asked for six stone jars, which could hold over twenty gallons each. He did not ask for clay jars, which could become unclean and contaminated according to Jewish tradition.

5. Read **John 2:6–12**. How does Jesus' miracle of turning water into wine display celebration and abundance?

6. How did the disciples respond to Jesus' first sign or miracle (Hint: verse 11)? How would you respond to seeing a similar miracle?

7. What does this scene communicate about Jesus' arrival on the world stage?

Just as Jesus provided an abundance of wine at a wedding celebration, so too does He offer an abundance of grace to us.

8. *Over the course of the next week, how can you intentionally celebrate the grace of God in your life?*

We can celebrate a life that reflects God's magnificent grace.

Digging Deeper

Just as God was the redeemer for the Israelites, who were delivered out of slavery in Egypt, Jesus came as the redeemer for the world. Read **Leviticus 25:47–49**. What similarities do you see between Jesus and the redeemer description in Leviticus? How does knowledge that Jesus is your kinsman-redeemer encourage you? Jesus didn't have to redeem us, but chose to do so. What do you find beautiful in that picture of grace?

Bonus Activity

Spend time celebrating the grace God has lavished on you. Select one or two hymns or worship songs that express praise for grace and commit them to memory. Play them in your car, at work, or at home as a consistent reminder to celebrate God's grace.

Leader's Guide

Chapter 1: Sufficient Grace

Focus: *From the very beginning, God lavished us with His grace. As we continue to grow in faith, we further understand God's grace as sufficient for our lives.*

1. *Answers will vary.* Merriam–Webster *defines grace as "unmerited divine assistance given humans for their regeneration and sanctification." Grace is also defined as "a special favor," "a disposition to or an act or instance of kindness," and "a temporary exemption."*[1] *Consider discussing these various definitions in addition to those developed by participants.*

2. *We are undeserving of the grace of God. Some find that a difficult truth to embrace. Grace is not something we can earn but a free gift of love and mercy from the Lord. No one deserves it. No one can earn it. Still, we should accept it with deep gratitude.*

3. *Eve was tempted by the edible nature of the fruit, its visual appeal, and the promise of wisdom. In our modern world, we face many parallel temptations. Sometimes we're tempted to eat things that literally aren't good for us. We may be tempted by how something looks, as when we buy a fashionable jacket we can't afford. We may also be tempted by the promise of worldly wisdom or knowledge, as in the case of reading a racy magazine article to learn how to lure as many admirers as possible. Rather than resting in the satisfaction of all God had given her, Eve was tempted by what she should not have. We all face a similar challenge.*

4. Eve responded to the serpent by claiming that she couldn't eat from the tree in the middle of the garden (which was true!), but she added that even if they touched it they'd die. The serpent promised that Eve's eyes would be opened and she'd know good from evil.

5. Be gentle and gracious to participants who share their struggles. Encourage them to find someone to hold them accountable. Remind them that we all fall, but God's grace meets us where we are and picks us back up. Even when we fall to temptation, God's grace is bigger than our mistakes. Our sin is not the end of the world. God is faithful to forgive and extend mercy to His children.

6. Paul was given a "thorn" as a constant reminder of his dependence on God. We all have limitations to remind us that we are dependent on God. They can take the form of sickness, financial challenges, relational difficulties, or even infertility.

7. God told Paul that His grace was sufficient for him because His power was made perfect in Paul's weakness. Answers will vary, but encourage participants to share their stories of God's grace in their weaknesses.

8. Instead of complaining about what we cannot do, we should take every opportunity to celebrate what the Lord can do through us despite our weaknesses. Encourage participants to share practical ways of celebrating their weaknesses, whether that's through being more honest about them, graciously accepting help from others, or thanking God for their struggle as well as their strengths.

Digging Deeper

When we learn to celebrate the grace of God and focus on the things He's given us (rather than those we don't possess), we can't help but grow more content. To be content in all circumstances is to receive the grace, joy, and sufficiency of God in all things. Contentment and graciousness often go hand-in-hand. Ultimately, Paul discovered that God is the source of all strength and contentment; we can find our strength and contentment in Him, too.

Chapter 2: Abundant Grace

Focus: *Sometimes we all need a reminder of God's grace—a grace that has no limits.*

1. *Encourage participants to share experiences of struggling and wondering about God's forgiveness in their own lives.*

2. *The son lives a life of irresponsibility and selfish desire. He squanders every last penny and ruins his family relationships. Encourage participants to share ways their attitudes and actions have been like the son's.*

3. *The son probably thought he would have to beg his dad for forgiveness and a job in the fields. He would have never expected his dad to be so welcoming and gracious.*

4. *The grace shown here seems unattainable. No father would let his son back that easily—or so it seems. Instead, we see a picture of abundant grace, reflective of the grace God extends to His children. Grace is available to all who'll receive it.*

5. The older son is upset and mad that the father accepted the younger son back. He doesn't understand grace, assuming the father should give only what's deserved. The problem is that no one, no matter their behavior or determination to do right things, deserves grace. We, too, put limitations on God's grace when we assume that people are too lost in sin to receive it.

6. Answers will vary.

7. Both brothers desperately needed to experience grace, though in very different ways. The younger brother needed his father's grace after making foolish decisions and squandering everything he had. The older brother needed his father's grace as he had become hard-hearted, serving out of a place of duty rather than delight.

8. How encouraging that no matter what we do, have done, or will do, the Lord will always extend grace to us. He pursues us constantly.

Digging Deeper

God's love is constant! We can always experience it. To have our sins removed from us as far as the east is from the west means God no longer sees our sin when He looks at us. How wonderful that through placing faith in the resurrection of Jesus we can walk in freedom and know that we are loved and accepted.

Chapter 3: Undeserved Grace

Focus: *As we begin to recognize and appreciate the grace God extends us, we can more fully extend contagious grace to those around us.*

1. *This question is designed to serve as a fun icebreaker. Remember, the quiz results are not meant to plumb the depths of participants' lives. Keep it fun!*

2. *The person may be quick to forgive, kind, humble, joyful, bubbly, sweet, thoughtful, or positive.*

3. *Self doubt, personal blame, and guilt can make us struggle to accept grace. When people wrong us multiple times, it becomes harder to extend grace. Christ's forgiveness knows no bounds. In striving to be more like Jesus, we must strive to show more grace.*

4. *Encourage honesty among participants by sharing from your own experiences.*

5. *The master forgives a massive debt out of compassion and graciousness. Share a time when someone was extremely gracious to you, even though you didn't deserve it.*

6. *The first servant owes his master the greater debt. This is ironic because that master forgave his servant and cancelled his debt, but the servant turned around and put the second servant into jail over his. The one forgiven should be the first to forgive.*

First Servant's Debt	Second Servant's Debt
The first servant owed his master ten thousand bags of gold.	The second servant owed the first servant only one hundred silver coins.

7. *Being able to receive grace is important because God's grace is readily available and saving. Being able to extend grace is crucial as it so well reflects the love of Christ toward others. Receiving grace makes it is easier to extend grace to others.*

8. *In order to be fully forgiven, we must habitually offer grace. Encourage participants to be intentional about extending forgiveness.*

Digging Deeper

Forgiving is difficult—especially when we feel wronged. We often try and justify unforgiveness, even though the Bible reminds us to forgive as the Lord forgives. In order to extend grace to one another, we must remember all the times God extends it to us—never withholding grace on the grounds we don't deserve it.

Chapter 4: Saving Grace

Focus: *We are saved by grace—God's saving grace is demonstrated through Jesus' sacrifice on the cross.*

1. *Encourage participants to share from their lists. Based on the time you have and the size of the group, encourage sharing less or more.*

2. *The jailer understood the power of Jesus and was shown grace just as he prepared to take his life.*

3. *Answers will vary. Remind participants that not everyone will have stories like the jailer in Acts, but that doesn't downplay the power of God's grace in each life.*

4. *Answers*

Scripture	Revelation about Salvation
Romans 3:23	Salvation is necessary. All have sinned.
Romans 6:23	Sin leads to death, but God offers eternal life through Christ.
1 John 5:11–13	God gives us eternal life through Jesus. With Jesus, we have life. Without Him, we don't.
1 John 1:9	If we confess our sins, we will be forgiven and purified from them.
Romans 10:9–10	If you profess and believe that Jesus is Lord, then you will be saved.

5. *God freely offers us His grace through Jesus. Just as we don't earn that grace at the moment of salvation, we cannot earn it in the day to day. We're dependent not on self effort but on God's endless generosity.*

6. *Some try following rules or "being a good person" in order to earn grace, but that is not how it works.*

7. *Encourage participants to explain why this sacrament is meaningful to them. Have your own reasoning ready to share.*

8. *Encourage participants to find three different activities through which they can remember salvation this week. Examples include taking communion, spending time in worship, and memorizing a passage of Scripture from this session. Encourage creativity and personal expression.*

Digging Deeper

The differences are small among these gospels. In the Luke account Jesus says, "Take this and divide it among yourselves" (22:17). The Matthew and Mark accounts use the same language. The Luke account seems to be the most different of the three but still communicates the same idea. Depending on the church denomination in which it's served, communion is treated in various ways. Encourage participants to share how they practice communion and how participation in the sacrament differs from the passages read.

Chapter 5: Grace Remembered

Focus: *Through the story of David and Mephibosheth, we see a picture of how the Lord extends grace to everyone—even the most unlikely and undeserving. Even to us.*

1. *Answers will vary.*

2. *David promises to show kindness, to give him back the land of his father Saul, and to invite him to eat at his kingly table. Answers will vary, but each of the kindnesses was amazing to Mephibosheth.*

3. *Answers will vary.*

4. *Mephibosheth shows David respect but asks, "What is your servant, that you should look upon such a dead dog as I?" (2 Samuel 9:8). It is not uncommon for us to feel unworthy of grace.*

5. *God's heart towards us is much like David's toward Mephibosheth. He is gracious to us because of Jesus' perfection—not because of anything we did. In us He sees not our mess-ups but lives made worthy and clean by our relationship with His Son.*

6. *Through Christ, not only have you experienced the kindness of God, you've been given an eternal inheritance and you are invited into an intimate relationship with the King of kings.*

7. *Answers will vary, but sometimes it is difficult to accept grace that we feel like we don't deserve. Encourage participants to thankfully receive God's gift.*

8. *Answers will vary. Consider relationships in the home, workplace, and church.*

Digging Deeper

To be holy is to be set apart. To be blameless means to be free from any condemnation or blame. Often we find it difficult to consider ourselves blameless or holy in any way, but that's how the Lord views us. In remembering the grace God gives us, we find it easier to strive toward holy living. Obeying God becomes a means of saying "thank you."

Chapter 6: Grace Strengthened

Focus: *Even when we feel at our weakest, God's grace is our source of strength.*

1. Samson was chosen by God to do great things but ended up falling into temptation. This fall was not the end of Samson's story; God still used him to defeat many of Israel's enemies.

2. Manoah desired to see more proof and pressed for further information. His wife believed immediately and followed the guidelines set.

3. Nazirites must abstain from wine, grape juice, or grapes. They must not cut their hair. They must not go near a dead body or make themselves unclean. If they see someone die in their presence, they must cut their hair and offer two birds to the priest. When their time of dedication is over, they must present offerings to the Lord. At the tent of meeting, they must shave their hair in order to represent dedication.

4. Answers

Scripture	Strength of Samson
Judges 15:8	He attacked and slaughtered several men.
Judges 15:15–16	He killed one thousand men with a donkey's jawbone.
Judges 16:3	He ripped out and carried the city gate.
Judges 16:6–9	He broke through seven bowstrings.
Judges 16:13–14	He pulled up the pin and the loom.

5. Answers will vary but Samson probably felt foolish, full of remorse and regret.

6. *We don't know exactly what compelled Samson to call on God. It may have been the desire to triumph over the Philistines one last time or to demonstrate the glory of God in their presence. What is clear is that Samson didn't give up on God's grace or ability to provide strength. God responded to his faith with grace, renewing Samson's strength and allowing him to kill more enemies in his final moments than in his entire life (Judges 16:30).*

7. *Samson didn't struggle just with lust but also with arrogance, anger, and pride. He made foolish choices in his relationships and didn't walk in wisdom. Samson had a weak character, but he knew God could use him even after his failures. He trusted God as the source of his strength.*

The second part of the question is designed to allow participants to get to know each other better as they discuss strengths and weaknesses. Examples of strengths may include persistence, timeliness, and organization. Examples of weaknesses may include pride, selfishness, and procrastination.

8. *God knows our weaknesses and understands our limitations. Through God alone, we can find strength when we can do nothing else on our own.*

Digging Deeper

It is encouraging that someone like Samson, who was easily tempted, can be still used by God. Despite our own weaknesses, God can still use us, too!

Chapter 7: Grace Recovered

Focus: *Grace is truly an amazing gift. When we stumble, we can recover through God's grace.*

1. This question is designed to encourage a discussion about grace recovered.

2. Gently encourage participants to share. Some participants may have yet to find healing for their mistakes. Pray with and for these participants who need healing from the Lord.

3. The opening line states that in "a time when kings go out to battle . . ." David chose not to join his men in battle. Likely the king had other things in mind—like giving himself a little break from responsibility.

4. The punishment for adultery was the death of both parties. David did not want to get caught breaking the rules he was supposed to protect. While we may say that his actions were unjustified, the truth is that we do similar things to try and cover up our mistakes.

5. David first tries to get Uriah to sleep with his wife, but his loyalty lies with the troops. Then, David has him placed at the front of the battle—a recipe for death.

6. Often we don't like to be held accountable, but accountability is one of the beautiful gifts of friendship. We are wise to search our hearts when lovingly confronted by a godly friend.

7. *Encourage participants to withhold names. Answers will vary, but prompt participants to prayerfully consider holding their own friends accountable–acting with humility and right intentions rather than in criticism that might be interpreted as self-righteousness.*

8. *We can find comfort in knowing that absolutely nothing can separate us from the redemption and love of God.*

Digging Deeper

The Lord used a relationship started in adultery to glorify Himself. Solomon would continue the line of kings that eventually led to Jesus.

Chapter 8: Grace Extended

Focus: *To begin receiving His magnificent grace, we must only call on God.*

1. *Answers will vary.*

2. *Peter probably was saddened. As we tend to do when confronted with our faults, he was probably motivated to prove his accuser wrong.*

3. *Peter cut off the high priest servant's right ear and continued following Jesus even after the arrest. This may have been Peter's attempt to show Jesus loyalty.*

4. *Peter didn't understand exactly what Jesus was accomplishing on earth at this point and was likely afraid of imprisonment and possible death.*

5. *Answers will vary. Peter probably wept out of remorse and regret.*

6. *Answers will vary, but we're reminded that despite Jesus' provision and generosity, we still have a part to play. Though we receive grace as a gift, we're still expected to serve as active participants in the story of God.*

7. *Peter jumped into the water and began swimming to shore. He left behind everything, including his boat and fellow disciples. Though Peter felt great remorse after his denial, his love for Christ continued with passion and verve.*

8. *Jesus can use anyone, even when we aren't fully committed. Through His grace, His power is made perfect despite our weaknesses and doubts.*

Digging Deeper

Peter gave a compelling sermon on how Jesus was in fact the Messiah. Peter was filled with confidence in the faith—people recognized that he had been with Jesus. Even though Peter denied Christ, he was still used by God to lead the early church.

Chapter 9: Healing Grace

Focus: *Part of not worrying about tomorrow means trusting that no matter what the next day brings, sufficient grace will be provided.*

1. *Gently encourage participants to share from their own experiences.*

2. *Insights will vary but may include discovering the depths of God's grace, the beauty of God's grace demonstrated through others, and the sense of God's grace despite difficult trials.*

3. *The disciples assume the reason for the man's blindness is sin— whether his parents' or the man's: they accept the cultural belief. Jesus shatters their misconception. He says the man was made blind not because of sin but so the work of God would be displayed in his life.*

4. *The man had mud placed on his eyes. A stranger told him to wash in a specific pool. When he returned home, his healing wasn't celebrated but interrogated. He was questioned by the most religious people he knew (Pharisees), only to be thrown out of the temple and then disregarded by his own family. All of these experiences must have been challenging.*

5. *The Pharisees tried to convince the man to proclaim the truth of retribution theology, the idea that physical malady is a result of sin. The blind man refused to concede, instead proclaiming what he knew to be true: he was blind but now could see. The Pharisees were more concerned with being right and upholding their cultural and religious beliefs than accepting the good news of Christ and the reality of His arrival through the testimony of miracles.*

6. *Jesus found the man and revealed Himself as the Messiah. Jesus wasn't just concerned with his physical sight but his spiritual sight.*

7. *Encourage participants to share from their own faith journeys about times when they experienced a shift in perspective or understanding from studying the Scriptures or by getting to know Jesus.*

8. *Encourage participants to share from their own lives. They may sense God in an opening of their eyes to social injustice and to the needs of the poor, or in a shift in the way they see, interact with, or serve Him.*

Digging Deeper

The passages are similar because they both deal with the healings of blind, begging men. They are different because of Jesus wanting to keep His identity quiet in one scene but not in the other. Bartimaeus was persistent in his desire to be healed and believed that Jesus could do it. His great faith healed him.

Chapter 10: Grateful Grace

Focus: *It's difficult to receive God's grace without a deep sense of gratitude.*

1. *Often we remember times when people thank us or express gratitude.*

2. *Things are done for us each day that may go unnoticed or unappreciated.*

3. *Often a lack of gratitude puts a bad taste in our mouths and can make us bitter.*

4. *The men asked for mercy and Jesus responded by showing them mercy. He instructed them to go to the priests, and they were cleansed as they obeyed.*

5. *Answers will vary. Only one of the men may have been truly grateful. Maybe he alone realized the source of his healing. Maybe the other nine were so excited they could go back to the city and their family members that returning home took priority over giving thanks.*

6. *Answers will vary.*

7. *Answers will vary, but many of us wrestle with all of these tendencies. We can remember to be thankful even when we're caught by surprise. When we forget, we can go back and offer thanks. A simple word of appreciation can go a long way. We can remember that all good things come from God, and He often uses people to deliver them. We can also learn to celebrate the small moments and gifts by saying thanks and recognizing that all roles are important.*

8. *Answers will vary, but we can lose our sense of gratitude toward God, family members, spouses, children, parents, grandparents, neighbors, churches, and in our workplaces when we fail to be intentionally thankful. Expressions of thanks can include affirming words, handwritten notes, gifts, and prayer.*

Digging Deeper

People who embody a spirit of thanksgiving usually are attuned to details, are kind, and will jump at the opportunity to help others. Encourage participants to share their psalms aloud.

Chapter 11: Generous Grace

Focus: *Abundant generosity fused with grace empowers us to share God's goodness at every turn.*

1. *It is inspiring that the Prince of Wales would take time to help someone of lower social stature. Encourage a fun discussion among participants as they recall similar stories.*

2. *Zacchaeus was a wealthy tax collector. He was physically short, but he was also fast since he ran ahead of the crowd to get a glimpse of Jesus. He was despised by the community.*

3. *The townspeople complained that Jesus associated with the sinner, Zacchaeus. Often, we make similar judgments about people we don't know or understand.*

4. *Answers will vary, but debt collectors still aren't warmly embraced. People make jokes and derogatory references about a long list of professionals: politicians, urban housing directors, lawyers, and real estate agents.*

5. *Zacchaeus offered to give up half of all he owned to the poor. On top of that, he promised to pay anyone he'd cheated four times as much as he'd stolen. Jesus responded by giving Zacchaeus salvation. Indeed, Jesus came to save that which was lost. Christ's offer was far more generous than Zacchaeus' offer, but the tax collector's generosity was an outward sign of the repentance taking place in his heart.*

6. *One can imagine the crowds flabbergasted by both responses. They were probably shocked that Zacchaeus would have such a change of heart, express such generosity, and offer to repay those he had cheated. He did this without Jesus asking him to do anything! But Jesus' immediately extending grace and offering salvation was even more extraordinary. If the Lord could accept Zacchaeus, He could accept anyone!*

7. *Answers will vary.*

8. *Answers will vary. We must take care not to overlook those who, like Zaccheaus, may not share our values but are curious about a relationship with Jesus.*

Digging Deeper

The nobleman represents Jesus. The servants represent Jesus' disciples. The servants who gain minas represent the disciples who go and develop what the Lord already has given them. The servant who simply buries the treasure represents disciples who decide to hide the good news they have been given and not share it with the world. The first two servants developed their gifts. The third lived unproductively. To His followers Jesus assigned the task of going and making disciples—not just resting on their blessings.

Chapter 12: Celebrating Grace

Focus: *We can celebrate a life that reflects God's magnificent grace.*

1. *This question is designed to encourage a fun discussion about the wonders and courage seen in trapeze and tightrope performances.*

2. *A person who "walks the tight rope" displays a life of active faith in Christ. They are likely characterized by love, forgiveness, mercy, and grace.*

3. *Though we often fall, God is faithful to extend grace. Encourage participants to share their moments of times when God extended grace after their tumbles.*

4. Jesus' mother tells the servants to do whatever Jesus says.

5. Jesus filled six jars with wine. This meant there were more than 120 gallons of wine for the celebration.

6. The disciples believed in Christ. Our responses may vary from disbelief to theological questioning to a joyful acceptance.

7. Answers will vary, but the miracle of turning water into wine speaks to the celebratory nature of Christ's arrival.

8. Encourage participants to share ways they can celebrate God's grace. Consider organizing a group activity to share God's grace with others.

Digging Deeper

Jesus came to redeem the world from the slavery of sin. He takes us on as His responsibility, paying the price for our failures. Knowing that Jesus is on our side and pulling for us is great encouragement worth celebrating. By God's grace, Jesus came to redeem us. We'll never deserve it, but we can spend our lives saying thanks!

Notes

Chapter 2

1. Adapted from Leslie B. Flynn, *Come Alive With Illustrations* (Grand Rapids: Baker Book House, 1988), 120–21.

Chapter 7

1. Adapted from Leslie B. Flynn, *Come Alive With Illustrations* (Grand Rapids: Baker Book House, 1988), 184.

Chapter 9

1. Source is an interview conducted by author with Michael Kelley on July 29, 2011.

Chapter 10

1. Adapted from Bill O'Brien, *The Christian Century*, June 28, 2005, 20.

Chapter 11

1. Adapted from John Ritchie, *500 Gospel Sermon Illustrations* (Grand Rapids: Kregel Publications, 1987), 58.

Chapter 12

1. Adapted from Juan C. Ortiz, "Words to Live By," http://www. eternalcog.org/wordstoliveby/1jn2_1.html.

Leader's Guide

1. *Merriam-Webster OnLine*, s.v. "grace," accessed July 9, 2011, http://www.merriam-webster.com/dictionary/grace.[2]

About the Author

A popular speaker at churches and leading conferences such as Catalyst and Thrive, Margaret Feinberg was recently named one of the "30 Voices" who will help lead the church in the next decade by *Charisma* magazine. She has written more than two dozen books and Bible studies, including the critically acclaimed *The Organic God*, *The Sacred Echo*, *Scouting the Divine*, and their corresponding DVD Bible studies. She is known for her relational teaching style and inviting people to discover the relevance of God and His Word in a modern world.

Margaret and her books have been covered by national media, including: CNN, the Associated Press, *Los Angeles Times*, Dallas Morning News, *Washington Post*, *Chicago Tribune*, and many others. She currently lives in Colorado, with her 6'8" husband, Leif, and superpup, Hershey. Go ahead, become her friend on Facebook, follow her on Twitter @mafeinberg, add her on Google+ or check out her website at www.margaretfeinberg.com.